Storm Tide

John Parker
Illustrated by Peter Foster

Rigby

Storm Tide

Rigby Heinemann
a division of Reed International Books Australia Pty Ltd
22 Salmon Street, Port Melbourne, Victoria 3207
World Wide Web http://www.rigby.com.au
Email info@hi.com.au

Offices in Sydney, Brisbane, Perth and Adelaide. Associated companies, branches and representatives throughout the world.

2005 2004 2003 2002 2001
10 9 8 7 6 5 4 3 2 1

Text by John Parker
Illustrated by Peter Foster
Designed by Andrew Cunningham

Typeset in New Baskerville
Printed by Impact Printing, Australia

National Library of Australia
ISBN 0 7312 3240 2

Contents

CHAPTER ONE

CAUGHT!

When Dan went down to the beach after lunch, he was going to fish from the dinghy. He planned to take it out a few metres from the shore. He would throw out the anchor in the shallows and then try his luck from there.

"But only if it's safe," his father had said. "And remember, always wear your life jacket."

Dan dropped his life jacket and fishing gear on the sand and looked at the sea. He didn't like it. The previous day's storm had vanished over the horizon but it had left dangerous water, cloudy with disturbed sand for two hundred metres out.

The waves were about eighty metres from the beach. They were big and lumpy. They changed direction suddenly, or rose unexpectedly.

Dan knew that a storm churned up the seabed. There would be food scraps for the fish. Schools of sprats would be swimming where there was clear water. Kingfish would be lurking in the cloudy water, ready to pounce. Big snapper would be feeding off crabs and shellfish left high and dry by the storm. It would have been good fishing.

But no way was Dan going to push out the dinghy into that water, even if the shallows were fifty metres or so from the waves—especially on an outgoing tide. It wasn't safe.

Still, Dan was disappointed. So was Putty. Dan patted the black labrador sitting beside him.

"No fishing today, Putty." The dog nuzzled Dan's hand. Her tail wagged.

Putty's brown eyes looked up at Dan. Then she got up and walked towards the rocks at the end of the beach.

It gave Dan an idea. He'd fish from the rocks, making sure he took no risks by staying well above any wave-splash once he made his cast. There might be a big fish mooching round the sides of the reef under the kelp. It was worth a try.

He wondered whether to put the life jacket back under the dinghy, then decided to take it with him. He could put it on while he was fishing. It would keep him warm.

Ten minutes later, he'd tied on his bait. He waited for a break between the waves, then ran to the end of the reef to cast out. His cast was good, even though it was only his short boat rod rather than the longer surf rod.

The strong wind was blowing offshore. It helped the bait go out beyond the reef and the long kelp into deeper water.

Dan ran back to his spot above the reef, letting the line spin out from the reel. But before he could put his life jacket on, the line jerked hard and pulled tight. Fish!

It took Dan ten minutes to reel it in to the side of the reef. It was a red snapper, the biggest he'd ever caught.

It would snap the line if he tried to haul it up and over the side of the rocks. He'd have to go down and scoop it out with his hands.

He checked the sea. It was calm enough. There were no big waves coming in. He could do it in thirty seconds. He scrambled to the edge of the reef and grabbed the tail of the flapping fish. Then Putty barked. It was a warning.

A wave had risen from nowhere. It reared above him. He had a moment to think how stupid he'd been, then it slammed down on the reef. Dan lost his footing. The wave foamed back into the sea. Dan went with it.

Dan's arms and legs stung as they scraped over the shellfish on the rock.

His right foot jammed for a half second in a hole in the reef. It came free, leaving his sneaker behind. Then he was fully in the water. The kelp swirled round him.

The water sloshed through his jeans and T-shirt and shocked his skin. The outgoing wave pulled Dan away from the reef and out to sea. He tried to grab onto the nearest rock as the current took him past, but his arms were tangled up in the rod and line.

The fish was still hooked. It throbbed through the line. It was pulling him down as it tried to swim deeper and away.

Then the rod caught in some kelp. The line tugged hard, then snapped. The fish swam off. Dan wrenched the rod away. At last he was free.

Dan looked at the rocks. He was shocked. They were seventy metres away! He knew there was a rip round the reef, but this was crazy! Each second, the rip and the outgoing tide took him further away.

It's the storm, he thought. All the storm water's going back to the sea in the outgoing tide. It's a storm tide as well as a rip, which makes it worse.

And I just happen to be right in the middle of it.

Scared, he swung his arms and legs in a frantic attempt to get back to the rocks. For twenty seconds, he put everything into it. Then, he looked up, gasping. He was no closer.

Dan tried to keep calm. He felt annoyed with himself. He'd got into a panic and just got tired for nothing. He'd have to wait. He'd have to be patient.

He remembered there was a man, a couple of years ago, who hadn't waited. Dan's dad wouldn't let him see the body when they'd brought him in. And for maybe a week afterwards, the beach and the sea seemed cool and unfriendly—even when the sun shone.

I'll have to go with the flow, thought Dan. I'll tread water. Maybe I'll move across the tide. I'll float a bit. Then I'll swim back in when the rip and the tide run out of steam.

He tried to keep calm but his heart ran faster. This storm tide was a mean one. It might take him three to four hundred metres, maybe more. It would be tough going getting back against the wind and outgoing tide.

Dan tried to swim diagonally across the rip. That would get him out of it faster. Relax, he said to himself as he swam. Just relax.

He stopped after a few minutes. His arms were tired. He looked back. The rocks were further away. Dan could see Putty running along the edge of the reef and then back again.

She was barking. She was worried about him. Good dog!

An idea came to him. If he waved Putty home, she might hightail it back to Mum and Dad and raise the alarm. She was a clever old thing.

Then they'd come down to the beach and realise what happened, Dan thought. Dad might be able to get through the surf and get me out of this mess. Worth a try. The less time I spend out here, the better.

He raised his right arm, then pushed his hand away from him, towards the shore. He repeated the sign. On dry land at home, Putty always knew what that meant. "Go away, Putty!"

On the reef, Putty got it all wrong. She barked more loudly. She paced up and down. Then she leapt into the sea.

Dan was angry with himself. Stupid again! He shouldn't have waved from so far away. It wasn't Putty's fault. It was his fault.

He hoped Putty wouldn't come to harm in the rough water. He hoped she'd swim across the rip, then back to shore.

Then he put Putty out of his mind. He had to think about himself. He tried to relax, going with the storm tide rather than fighting it.

How long had he been in the water? He looked at his watch. It had stopped. He shook it hard. The hands remained still. Just a cheap watch, thought Dan. He made a guess at the time. He thought it was about thirty minutes since the wave had swept him off the reef.

How far out was he? He looked back at the shore, but couldn't see it until a swell lifted him. If I find it hard to see the beach, Dan thought, then it'll be harder still for someone to see me out here in the sea.

He reckoned he was about three hundred metres out. He thought the rip was slowing, but there was nothing to measure the flow against. Dan told himself not to worry. The rip was taking longer to stop because it was running on a storm tide. It was just the sea doing its natural thing.

But doubts wormed their way into Dan's mind. That strong wind was coming off the shore. He was already feeling cold, even though it was late summer. Deep water was colder than shallow water, Dan was discovering.

Out of habit, he looked at his watch again, then remembered it was dead. Suddenly, really annoyed, he wrenched it off and threw it away. Its white face gleamed for a few seconds, then it sank out of sight.

Dan told himself to be calm again, not to waste his energy. Why be angry about a stupid watch?

Another thought wormed in. The watch was on its way to the bottom.

Other eyes might be looking at it as it sank. Suddenly, he felt alone in a watery place where the only rule was eat or be eaten.

He felt the scrapes on his legs and arms. They'd stopped stinging, but they were still bleeding. He tried not to think about the little trail of blood around him, spreading out into the sea. He tried not to think of the word that made his feet feel like live bait inviting a bite.

But he couldn't help it. Shark.

Dan decided to float on his back with his arms and legs stretched out. That way, he'd save on energy and maybe on warmth, too. If there was something watching from below, having his legs on the surface made him feel safer.

It didn't work out nearly as well as he'd hoped. He wasn't able to see where the next wave was going to come from and sometimes, the water slopped into his eyes and made them sting. They were red with salt. There was glare from the sun, as well.

So Dan kept them shut most of the time—but that made him feel giddy as he floated on the swell. Still, he kept at it, telling himself he had less than an hour to go. Then he could swim for shore on the in-going tide.

After twenty minutes, he tried a different way of floating. His dad had told him about it. He tucked himself into a ball with his knees up to his chest and allowed himself to sink. He breathed out while underwater. When his lungs emptied, he rose.

He helped himself the last few centimetres with a small push downwards with his hands. It was just enough to get his mouth into the air. Then he'd take a deep breath and do it all again.

It was better than floating on his back. But once, when he came up for a mouthful of air, he swallowed a splodge of water that the wind and a wave had pushed into his face.

He choked and fought for his breath for a couple of minutes. He had to tread water until he'd coughed it all out.

It took a long time for his lungs to come right. He felt small and helpless in the middle of tonnes of uncaring water.

After all the coughing, he felt colder. He pushed the skin of his arm with his fingers. It was soft and wrinkly, as if he'd stayed in the bath too long.

He tried to estimate how long he'd been in the water by how low the sun was. It was harder than he thought. After a while, he stopped trying and decided to start swimming instead. Surely the tide would be weakening. He had to stop being pushed around by this sea. He had to do something.

He remembered one of his mum's favourite sayings. When the going gets tough, the tough get going.

He had better be tough and push for the shore. He concentrated on keeping his stroke loose and relaxed. He used his legs in a slow kick rather than beating up the water like an outboard motor.

Don't rush it, he thought. Keep it slow. You've got a long way to go.

He wondered if his parents would be worried. Probably not, he thought. Sometimes he'd stay out on the boat for a couple of hours.

To keep himself going, he thought of good things. He pictured himself eating a big dinner with his mum and dad. Putty would be sitting at his feet. Her tail would be thumping the floor.

The pictures evaporated when he caught sight of something orange about thirty metres away. It was turning over on top of the water.

It was his life jacket.

Dan stopped swimming and stared at it. He couldn't believe it. How did it get there? He'd left it above the waterline. Then he realised—the wind would have blown it off the rocks and into the water. And here it was.

For a few seconds, he thought he'd let it drift past him and away. It would be hard swimming with a life jacket. He might be better off without it, especially when he'd have to swim away from the shore to get it.

Then, a wave slapped his face and he swallowed more water. He choked for a few seconds. It made him feel unsafe and lonely. Suddenly, he wanted the jacket, badly. The sea was giving him a chance. He had to grab it.

He turned to go after the jacket, but he couldn't see it. He swam to where he last saw it—but there was no sign. He thought he'd lost it. Then it floated up on top of a wave. It was still thirty metres away.

"Stay still!" Dan screamed. He put everything into the chase. His heart raced. His legs and arms churned up the water. At last, his hand clutched the jacket. He felt triumphant. The jacket would keep him warmer and help him stay afloat.

He felt confident again. His hand punched the air. "Yes!" Dan yelled to the sun and the sky.

It was a struggle to get the jacket on, but it made a big difference. He felt like a cork, not like something that wanted to sink.

Dan tightened the cord, then turned again for the shore. Chasing the jacket had cost him time. He had to make the beach before dark.

He swam on for about twenty minutes. He sensed that the tide was turning and beginning to favour him—but the wind was still against him. It slopped blobs of water into his eyes and face. He had to be careful when he breathed, in case he took in some sea as well.

"You're a darn nuisance, wind!" shouted Dan. He banged the water with his fist. "And you're a stupid sea! Do you hear that, sea! Stupid!"

Dan's lungs heaved. He gasped as he had when he first tried to get out of the current. You're the stupid thing, he told himself. Now, keep calm.

A new sound came to him. It was different. It was something alive and splashing and coming his way.

The next moment, he saw a black shape in the water. He could see the legs working hard. The ears craned forward. The nose lifted out of the water. The shape barked. It was Putty.

CHAPTER TWO

SURPRISE!

Dan's father put away the lawnmower. He smiled as he looked at the neat lawns and edges and sniffed the nice smell of mown grass.

Perhaps he and Dan could have some fun on the lawn with a bat and ball. He wondered how Dan was doing out in the boat. He knew his son wouldn't go out unless it was safe. He was a sensible boy.

He looked at his watch. It was 5 o'clock, later than he thought. Dan should have been back an hour ago.

His wife was doing the weekly shopping. He thought of ringing her on her mobile—then pictured her struggling with the phone at the checkout. No, he wouldn't bother her.

He went inside, and turned on the TV to watch the sports. He couldn't settle to it, though. He felt worried about Dan. Perhaps he should have gone with him to check the conditions.

He switched off the TV and walked down to the beach. On the way, he tried to think for the best. Maybe Dan was landing so many fish, he'd decided to stay out longer. Maybe he was cleaning the fish or just relaxing in the sun with Putty.

But Dan's father didn't feel happy. He started running.

Putty's nose pushed into Dan's face. She licked him. Her hard paws thrust against his life jacket. She gazed at him with love.

Putty's black coat was bedraggled and sopping—but her first thought was for Dan's safety.

Dan's throat was lumpy when he saw her, but she was a problem. He'd hoped Putty would be raising the alarm back home. Here she was, trying to rescue him!

Now he had to get her back as well as himself. That would not be easy. But he shook the thought away. He had to keep strong. "We'll get back, Putty," said Dan. "No worries!"

Putty's tail wagged a little in reply. Then she pointed her nose to the shore and started paddling. Dan kept close alongside.

As he swam, he thought of something his dad had said once when he and Putty had been splashing in the shallows. "Don't go swimming too far out with Putty." When Dan had asked him why, his father had answered,

"Because swimming dogs can attract sharks."

Shark. The word squirmed into Dan's mind again. It made him want to draw his legs up to his chest and curl up his toes. He shook his head, trying to push the scared feeling away. He just had to keep on swimming. He and Putty. They had to make it before night.

Even before Dan's father reached the beach, he spotted the dinghy lying on the sand in its usual place above the high water mark.

He could see why Dan had left it. Those waves would be too tough for any small boat. He ran over to it and looked underneath. The oars were still there, but there was no life jacket.

It was strange. Why was the life jacket missing? Where were the boat rod and the bait bag?

Maybe Dan had met up with a friend from one of the other beach-side houses, thought his father. It didn't ring true, though. Even if he had, Dan would surely have been back before now.

The houses were empty, anyway. The drawn curtains and shut windows showed that. Most owners would have stayed away because of the storm.

Dan's father sat down on the boat and tried to think it out. Maybe Dan had put on the life jacket first. Then he would have decided not to fish because of the waves—but he would have been disappointed. So he would probably have gone fishing from the rocks.

That's where he'd be. Dan's father snapped his fingers. Yes!

For the first few metres, he walked to the rocks. Then he started to run again. When he rounded the corner, he could see the length of the reef.

It was almost dead-low tide, but there was no sign of Dan.

The rocks and reef were covered with brown seaweed and long kelp. The water sucked in and out of the rock pools as it surged over the edges, then flowed out again to the sea.

Dan's father saw a seagull picking at something on the rocks higher up, away from the tide-line. He scrambled up. The seagull flew away, squawking.

Dan's bait bag was ripped to pieces, the plastic torn by seagulls. There were shreds of bait, some crusts of bread. Dan's tackle box lay unopened.

Dan's father opened it. It was untouched. He saw hooks, sinkers, traces, a spinner, an unwrapped candy bar. But where was the boat rod?

He walked down to the rocks closer to the sea. Some of them were greasy-green with moss. One rock was too slippery for him. He sprawled on his hands and knees. It hurt.

He was about to rub the sore bits, when he stiffened in shock. Right in front of him were a boat rod and reel—the set they'd bought Dan for Christmas. He picked up the rod. He tried to make sense of the broken line and the scratched reel.

He observed the sea again. It was a dirty sea. The kind of sea that might surprise a boy who was bending down trying to catch a fish that he'd landed on the rocks.

He ran round the reef. Sometimes he slipped and fell but he scarcely noticed the bruises. He peered over the edges into the sucking kelp as it rose and fell with the restless waves.

He saw one of Dan's sneakers was jammed in a crevice. He reached down and grabbed it. His hands trembled. He didn't see what he feared most—the sight of Dan's body caught in the long kelp.

He straightened up and gazed out to sea. He was sure Dan was out there, somewhere, caught by the storm tide. Somehow he had to get the dinghy through the waves and find him.

He scrambled across the rocks to the beach, then sprinted up the sand towards the dinghy. Another thought puzzled him as he ran. What could have happened to Putty?

CHAPTER THREE

TOUGH GOING

Dan's arms and legs were so tired he had to stop swimming. He rested in the water for a moment, bobbing around in the swell.

For a few seconds, Putty paddled on. Then she swam back to him. She's like a sheepdog, Dan thought. I'm her sheep and she's herding me back to land. The trouble was, Dan knew it was the other way around. He was a shepherd in charge of a dog. Putty was tiring. She was swimming more slowly. Her body was shivering. Dan didn't wonder. He was cold enough even with his life jacket. His hands were more yellow-white than brown.

Putty needed food to give her energy, but dog biscuits were a million miles away. Dan's stomach stabbed in hunger. He could kill for a hamburger!

He also felt thirsty. It was strange to want liquids in the middle of tonnes of the stuff. He wished he had a magic wand and a long pointed hat. He'd say, "Abracadabra!" and turn the sea into chocolate milkshake.

Or else, he'd magic up a big bed that he and Putty could lie on. It would have an outboard, too. They'd put it on auto-pilot and head for the beach. His mum and dad would be on the beach with a warm sleeping-bag all ready for him. They'd be sizzling sausages on the barbecue. He closed his eyes at the wonderful thought.

He felt drowsy. He wanted to rest and float around in the life jacket. What was the point of this silly swimming? He could drift for months like a piece of wood.

He felt a paw poke his chest. Putty was looking at him urgently. She let out a breathy woof. Get going, she was saying. You can't stay here.

Dan wearily turned his face to the shore. Putty was so right. There was less light now. It was definitely fading. They had to keep going. It was still a long way—maybe half-a-kilometre.

The offshore wind slapped his face as he and Putty kept at it.

Dan's father pushed the boat off from the shore. He had studied the wave patterns. The big ones were coming in three at a time. Then there would be smaller ones. If he could avoid the big waves, he'd have a chance.

It was quite difficult keeping the boat square-on to the waves, though.

The water wanted to slew it sideways. He dug in with his oars as he tried to keep the boat moving forward and in a good position.

He craned his neck around as he got closer to the break. The dinghy bobbed like a frisky horse. Keeping it balanced and steady was getting more and more difficult.

Then Dan's father saw a chance. Now! He strained his back, gritted his teeth, stretched his arms, and drove hard with his legs as he muscled the boat forward.

He rowed between two waves and thought he was through. But a rogue wave pushed diagonally off one that had just passed. It rose underneath the dinghy. The small boat slid down the crest and flipped over.

It happened in slow motion, but Dan's father could do nothing except grab the anchor rope as he fell out.

Dan's father waded back to shore, hauling the boat behind him. He'd lost precious time in his search for his son. He clenched his fists and yelled in frustration. Then he heard a voice.

"William! What's the matter?"

He turned to his wife and ran towards her.

Dan couldn't believe how tired he was. Yet he kept on going. His neck was stiff. His eyes stung so sharply that he could only squint. Much of the time he kept them shut, getting his direction from the wind on his face.

Putty moved her legs tightly and jerkily. She was staying closer to Dan.

Sometimes, Dan held her with one arm. Then he had to swim sidestroke with one arm. It was slow going.

For a while, Dan tried swimming on his back, trying to keep himself on course by keeping the sun behind him. It was easier on his neck, but the waves slopped into his face and eyes.

He was colder. His muscles weren't working smoothly. He guessed his body temperature was dropping too low. He willed his muscles to keep going. When the going gets tough, the tough get going.

His mind was slow. He had trouble remembering whether the tide was going in or out. Was his mind giving up, like his muscles?

He tested himself as he swam. What was his dad's middle name?

Joseph. Who was the tallest girl in his class? Sophie. What was the motto of his school? Always do your best.

Always do your best, thought Dan. That's what I'm doing here—but Putty and I wouldn't be in this mess if I hadn't been stupid. He thought of a better school motto. Beware the storm tide!

He daydreamed as his arms and legs slowly turned and kicked. What would Mum and Dad be doing? What would that snapper be doing? What if the sky turned into sea and the sea turned into sky? Then he'd be swimming miles above the sea—except he couldn't because the sea was now the sky. It was very confusing.

Something alerted him. Putty had stopped paddling. She gave a low warning bark. She stuck her head under water and turned it from side to side as if watching something.

Dan's mother looked at the waves. "I think they're dropping," she said. "I reckon we can do it."

Dan's father watched the waves for a few minutes. Yes, he thought, they're definitely smaller.

He looked at the clouds. The wind had shifted. It was now coming back to shore. That would have helped to flatten the waves. The incoming tide would have done the rest.

The ebbing storm tide and the off-shore wind had kept the waves up high so that they reared and dumped. Now that the tide and wind had changed, they could get out there and start searching before night came.

He turned to his wife. "I'll row. You steer with the spare oar. Call out when there's a calm patch. Let's go!"

Putty lifted her head. She put it under the water again. She gave a warning woof like the sound she'd make at home if she sensed an intruder. Dan's skin prickled. He knew Putty picked up things before he could. Dogs were sharp—especially Putty. She was tracking something under the water—just as it was tracking them.

Dan's blood ran cold. He knew that dawn and dusk were good times for catching fish—and good times for fish to catch other fish.

It's a shark, thought Dan. It's coming in at dusk to see if we're good to eat or not. Oh no!

CHAPTER FOUR

THE LAST TEST

Dan was tempted to swim on. Instead, he moved as fast as he could to Putty. He had to protect her. The bigger the prey it was hunting, the more cautious a shark would be.

He and Putty had to look like something big and together. An old plump labrador on its own would be easy meat—picked off and torn to bits in a few seconds.

He held Putty with one arm. She kept dipping her head in the water trying to see the thing that was watching her. The hairs on the ridge of her back bristled. She growled.

Dan's legs trembled. He wished he had wings, so he could fly off and carry Putty to safety.

Then Putty relaxed. The hairs on her back flattened. She stopped looking under the water. Maybe that thing under the water wasn't a shark, Dan thought. Maybe it was a dolphin.

Dan began to swim again—as smoothly as he could. He knew that anything that smelt of panic would attract a shark. They were closer to the shore. Dan could see the backs of the waves ahead as they began to rise towards the beach.

There was no spray coming off them. The wind had turned. Now it was behind them. Dan felt hope. He and Putty were going to make it. Only twenty minutes, maybe thirty, to go.

Then Putty trembled. Her back hairs rose again. Dan's heart jolted. The thing was back again. Somehow he knew it would return. The sea had kept the biggest danger of all till last.

Dan felt so helpless. What was it? Where was it? How big was it? He had so many questions but only the sea knew the answers—and it wasn't telling him anything.

He never stopped swimming, though. "Come on, Putty," he kept on saying. "It's okay. Keep going, Putty."

He held Putty close, moving slowly and regularly. He wanted the shark to think they were a big powerful fish cruising through the sea, just minding its own business—and expecting all the other fish to mind theirs.

Dan scanned the water. He thought he saw something bulge briefly near the top of a wave, about twenty metres away. It wasn't a fin, more an impression of something big and solid pushing up the water.

What was it? Where was it? Was it anything at all?

Dan put his head under the water. Even in the gloom, there was no mistaking it—a big hammerhead, five metres in front of him.

Dan did the bravest thing in his life. Holding tightly to Putty, he swam straight at the shark. It flicked past him. Dan lost it in the water, then he saw it again, a dim shape to his left, on the edge of his vision.

It came at them again, with a lazy power. Dan faced it. The shark was the king of the sea. Dan and Putty were intruders in its domain. Yet, once again, it turned away.

I need a weapon, Dan thought. He could only think of his sneaker. He pulled it off and held it in front of him.

When the shark came at them from the right, Dan stretched out his arm and waggled the sneaker. He thought it was about as useful as trying to stop a tanker with a banana skin, but he had to do something.

The hammerhead circled closer. As it approached, Dan remembered a story he'd read in a newspaper about a diver who'd blown bubbles at a shark in a last effort to scare it away.

Dan took a deep breath and blew noisily into the water in front of the shark. He shook the sneaker. He snorted. With a lightning flick of its tail, the hammerhead disappeared.

The bubbles and snorting were too much for Putty. She kicked against Dan and broke away from his grasp. Then, a wave washed her away. Within ten seconds, she was twenty metres away.

Within thirty seconds, he'd lost sight of her in the dim early-evening light. Her black coat made it impossible to see her. She was gone—and that hammerhead would finish her off.

Dan yelled in despair. "Putty! Putty!"

She barked in reply. She barked a second time. Then there was an awful silence.

Dan wanted to sob. The hammerhead had got her. He had to keep swimming, though, for Putty's sake. She'd sacrificed herself for him.

Dan looked around. The shore was much closer now. He could hear the waves. Soon he'd have to go over them to get to the beach. He did not know how he was going to do that.

But he'd face that problem when he came to it. One thing at a time. At least the tide and the wind were with him, now.

Suddenly, Dan heard a shout. Was it someone on the shore? Someone on the water? He had no idea. He began to force his legs and arms into a final effort.